SCHOLASTIC

Instant DESKTOP ORGANIZER

TEACHER HANDBOOK

—•—

Everything You Need to Manage & Keep Track of Your Paperwork—All Year Long!

by Barbara Gruber & Sue Gruber

NEW YORK • TORONTO • LONDON • AUCKLAND • SYDNEY
MEXICO CITY • NEW DELHI • HONG KONG • BUENOS AIRES

Teaching *Resources*

For busy teachers everywhere

Cover design by Maria Lilja

Interior design and artwork by Sydney Wright

ISBN: 0-439-66754-2

Copyright © 2004 by Barbara Gruber & Sue Gruber

Published by Scholastic Inc.

Printed in China.

16 17 18 19   62   18 17 16 15

Contents

Introduction

Every teaching day is a race against the clock—there's never enough time to fit everything into each packed school day! Every minute is precious, and nothing eats up more valuable time than disorganization. How much time do you spend each week searching for "lost" items? Wouldn't you rather use that time teaching, planning, or actually eating your lunch? Your Instant Desktop Organizer gives you specific places to put all those important papers and reminder notes that accumulate each and every school day. You'll be *organized*!

The benefits are huge. Take a look at what you have to gain:

- You'll have more time—no more frantic searches for important papers.

- You'll get more accomplished.

- You'll have less stress.

- You'll be less frustrated and more enthusiastic.

- Your level of enthusiasm correlates with how much children learn—everyone wins!

- Your job becomes easier and more fun!

You'll wonder how you ever taught without this valuable tool— your Instant Desktop Organizer!

Instant Desktop Organizer

Every teacher has piles of papers to manage. The Instant Desktop Organizer is *the* best system for paper management! It helps you get organized quickly—and stay that way. This organizational tool works at all grade levels and in all kinds of classrooms.

Take a look at the file folder labels included and choose the ones that work for you. Here are some suggestions for making the most of each folder:

DO TODAY

Put all papers that relate to things you have to do *before leaving school today* in this folder. Don't let yourself leave school until you've taken care of everything in here. Before you leave for the day, transfer everything from your Do Tomorrow folder into the Do Today folder. Now you're organized for tomorrow. Check your Do Today folder the minute you walk in the door each morning. You'll feel focused and ready to go!

Tip!

Make copies of the lists on page 19 on brightly colored paper. Cut apart the lists and keep several blank ones inside the Do Today folder so they are ready to use.

DO TOMORROW

It's easier to use your time wisely when you know exactly what you have to do and when it needs to be completed. Put everything you need to do tomorrow in here.

DO BY FRIDAY

Work has a way of piling up as the week unfolds! Slip everything that needs to be attended to by Friday into your Do by Friday folder. Set up a standing "date" with this folder every Friday during your first recess or prep time.

READ LATER

You've just come back from the office with a catalog you want to look through later, plus a copy of an interesting article. Don't lose them in the classroom—put them in your Read Later folder. Take the folder with you to lunch every week or two, or when you're waiting for appointments.

TAKE TO OFFICE

Do you have a birthday card for the most important person in the school, also known as the school secretary? How about administrative paperwork that you need to bring to the office? Pop them in this folder so you don't forget to take them on your next trip!

TAKE HOME

Anything you need to bring home goes in this folder. Use it for papers you need to grade at night, lesson plan forms to fill out, or things you've decided to keep at home rather than school.

CLASS LIST

Keep a list of students, family contact information, birthdays, and so on, here. You can also keep grade information in this folder. In addition, you might make extra copies of your class list. You'll have ready-to-go lists of children's names—sure to come in handy.

TO PHOTOCOPY

Make fewer trips to the copy machine! Put everything that needs to be copied in here, then do all your copying at once.

TO FILE

Here you can organize paperwork that needs to make it back into your file cabinet. Every week or two, spend a few minutes at your file cabinet emptying this folder.

TAKE TO MEETINGS

No more frantic searches for papers you need for upcoming meetings! Keep all of the paperwork for staff meetings and committee meetings in this folder.

Tip!

Pop a few extra blank copies of the lists on page 19 into the To File folder file. They just might come in handy during a meeting!

Instant Desktop Organizer

Use the blank labels to customize your desktop organizer. Once you're in the habit of using your organizer, you'll think of additional ways to make it work best for you. Take a look at these ideas:

NEXT WEEK

Is your materials request form due next week? A book order? Keep the paperwork in this folder.

NEXT MONTH

Are you going on a field trip next month? Do you have a class visitor scheduled? Put all the pertinent paperwork in here. During the last week of each month, transfer the papers to the appropriate folders.

NOTES TO WRITE

Place notes and letters that require a written response in this folder so they don't get lost or forgotten.

PHONE CALLS TO MAKE

How many times have you searched your desk for a phone number written on a scrap of paper? Stash everything that relates to calls you need to make, and those you need to return, in this folder. Pop a copy of your class list with students' phone numbers inside this file.

PENDING

You've sent off your book order, or you're waiting for a response to a note. Place your copy of the paperwork in this folder.

WORK TO BE CORRECTED

Clip batches of papers together by subject, and place them in this folder to be corrected later. You might also keep a few extra sheets of stickers here to use for grading work.

WORK TO BE RECORDED

When recording corrected work, why not color code your entries? For example, record homework grades in pencil, classwork in black pen, and tests in red.

SUBSTITUTE INFORMATION

Include a copy of the form on page 25 in this folder. Include an extra copy of your class picture in this folder.

DAY-AT-A-GLANCE

Designate one folder for each school day (labeled Monday–Friday). Place everything you'll need for each day in this folder. If there are materials you didn't have time to use during the week, pop them into your substitute folder. They'll come in handy when you are planning for a sub.

NEXT YEAR

Keep a blank Year-at-a-Glance Planner form (pages 22–23) handy in this folder. Every time you get an idea you want to try next year, write it down and put it here.

Organize the Clutter Zones

Sometimes the hardest part of any task is getting started. Simply follow these steps to a more organized you.

> ⚙ First, select the area that you most want to get organized.
>
> ⚙ Break the task into manageable chunks. Don't worry about getting everything done in one session.
>
> ⚙ Visualize the results of your efforts.
>
> ⚙ Jot the steps you need to take on a list. Then immediately do the first thing on the list.
>
> ⚙ Reward yourself when you complete the project.

As you sort through all the clutter, question the value of every item you touch. Ask yourself if each item is something you really need. Make sorting easy by labeling six empty boxes:

- Discard
- Goes Somewhere Else
- Stays Here
- To Be Filed
- Belongs to Someone Else
- Can't Decide What to Do With It

❖ Get rid of the Discard box by tossing the entire box in the trash or recycling.

❖ Place the box of things to be filed on top of your file cabinet. You can deal with it later.

❖ Find homes for all the objects in your Goes Somewhere Else box.

❖ Return the contents of the Belongs to Someone Else box to their owners. Chances are you found at least one thing that belongs to someone else!

❖ Carefully place everything in your Stays Here box according to how often you need access to it. Items used on a daily basis need to be kept handy. Store occasionally used items out of sight. For instant access, label everything! Now you can find things at a glance without wasting time sifting through unlabeled boxes and containers.

❖ The things in your Can't Decide box clearly aren't essential items. Take a deep breath and ruthlessly sort through the items one more time! Store items you just can't bear to part with.

CONQUER YOUR CLOSET

When you open your closet, are you hit with an avalanche of cascading papers, charts, and boxes? It's time for a closet overhaul! Take everything out of your closet and put it back together—the organized way!

Check out these nifty organizers for your closet:

Over-the-door hanging shoe bags: Buy two shoe-bag organizers— hang one inside and one outside your closet door. Store your keys, coffee mug, snacks, supplies (for your use only), whistle, school ID card, and so on, on the inside of the door. The shoe bag on the outside of the door is perfect for storing items students need access to, such as art supplies, scissors, and calculators.

Hanging baskets: Hang a three-tiered wire basket from the rod in your closet. Instantly, you have three baskets at the perfect height for easy-access storage! See-through wire mesh baskets make it easy to quickly grab whatever you need.

Hooks: Maximize your options by adding a row of hooks (either screw-in or stick-on) to your closet.

Space-saver skirt hangers: Skirt hangers with tiers of clips are ideal for storing charts! Simply clip charts onto the hanger and hang it in your closet.

Tall plastic wastepaper basket: Pop your yardstick and rolled charts into a tall waste-paper basket in the corner of your closet. Secure rolled charts with clothespins.

Last but not least, customize your closet:

- Make a closet survival kit. Gather all the essential items you need to make it through just about anything! Pop these items in a box or in the pockets of your shoe-bag organizer: pocket change, Band-Aids, lip balm, candy, a mini first-aid kit, instant coffee, tea or hot chocolate, hand lotion, toothbrush and toothpaste, tennis shoes, blank birthday cards, thank-you notes, and so on.

- Hang a mirror at just the right height inside your closet door. Teaching can be just plain messy at times!

- Post favorite cartoons, pictures, and cards inside your closet door for an instant lift when you need it.

- Brighten a dark closet with an inexpensive, stick-on, battery-operated light!

ORGANIZE YOUR DESK

Is your desk a place where you can really sit and get some work done? Are your supplies neatly stored? Chances are your desk is buried in a mountain of papers. Make your desk into a workspace that is organized and personalized.

The first step is the purge. Empty your desk and ask yourself these questions about desk contents:

- ✓ Does this belong in my desk?
- ✓ Am I really attached to it?
- ✓ Is this easy to find elsewhere?
- ✓ Do I have room for this?
- ✓ Is it something that I will really use?

- ✓ Do I need this?
- ✓ Is this a duplicate?
- ✓ Is this old and outdated?
- ✓ Is it relevant to my current job?

Sort items into piles, such as:

- ◎ Things to Discard
- ◎ Things to Take Home
- ◎ Things That Go Elsewhere in the Classroom
- ◎ Things to Return to Others
- ◎ Papers to File
- ◎ Things I Use Often and Need in or on My Desk

Get rid of the discard pile immediately before you start to "rescue" things you don't really need! Throw everything in your take-home pile into a box or bag to take home. Find homes for everything in your pile of things that go elsewhere in the classroom. Put everything that needs to be returned to others in a box near your classroom door. You can start passing things back to their owners tomorrow during recess or lunch. Label a box "To Be Filed" and fill it with everything that needs to make its way back into your file cabinet. Put the box on top of your file cabinet to tackle later.

It's time to set up your organized desk:

❖ Everything you put back on your desk should be placed in a specific spot. It's easy to keep your desk organized if you have places for everything! You can even label the spots on the desktop where things belong.

❖ Keep clutter to a minimum. Do you have a lot of decorative gifts from students? Designate a windowsill to display your knickknack hall of fame.

❖ Items you use frequently should be kept at the ready. Those items you rarely use can be stashed in a drawer out of sight. You want to have access to everything quickly and easily. If it's inconvenient to retrieve an item, you won't use it and you certainly won't want to put it away!

You'll need these desk essentials:

⊛ Trash and/or recycling containers

⊛ Office supplies (paper clips, pushpins, staples and stapler, staple remover, pens, pencils, pencil sharpener, correction fluid or correction tape, envelopes, sticky notes)

⊛ A comfortable chair, preferably one that swivels

⊛ A hook for your keys. A magnetic hook is perfect to attach to a metal desk. If your desk is wooden, screw in a small hook as a key holder. Or place it inside the legroom section of your desk.

⊛ An extra chair or two, if you plan to meet with parents or students at your desk

The more space you create, the easier it is to keep your desk organized. Try these ideas to maximize the surface area of your desk:

❖ Push an empty student desk next to your desk. Ask the custodian to adjust the height of the extra desk so that it's level with your desk. You might want a desk on each side. Students can sit at these desks when you are helping them.

❖ Place an empty table behind your desk. It's easy to access this space if you have a desk chair that swivels. With a twist of your chair, you have a large work surface that's perfect to use for planning and for projects you need to spread out.

❖ A two-drawer file cabinet next to your desk provides an additional work surface and is handy for the files you use most.

CONTROL YOUR FILE CABINET

The tricky part about file cabinets is retrieving the items that you've filed. Follow these suggestions to make your file cabinet organized and user-friendly!

Sort by Month and Time of the School Year . . .
It's easy to get started—all you need is a stack of empty file folders. Label them:

- Before School Starts
- First Week of School
- Back-to-School Night
- Fall Projects/Activities
- Parent Conferences
- Winter Projects/Activities
- Spring Projects/Activities
- Open House
- Last Week of School
- Parent Communication
- One file folder for each month of the school year

. . . Or, Sort According to Skills
Color-code your files to identify curriculum areas such as reading, writing, math, science, and art. Make file folders for each of the specific skills you teach in each content area. Now you can instantly get your hands on the ideas you need. For example, rather than sorting through a bulging file labeled "Word Skills," it's easier to open a Compound Words file and be ready to go. Identify and sort through files that are too general and break them down skill by skill. Add worksheets and articles about specific skills from teaching magazines. Photocopy ideas from books, and put them in the appropriate skills files.

Top Five Tips for File Cabinet Success

1 Use a yellow highlighter to label original copies of reproducible worksheets "Master" or "Original." The highlighted word won't show when you copy it and you'll never give away your master by mistake.

2 Write the name of the file from which each idea and worksheet came on the lower right-hand corner of the page. It's a breeze to file items when you've marked where they go! Once you identify papers, a volunteer helper can do your filing for you.

3 Does a favorite unit take up too much file cabinet space? If, for instance, your dinosaur unit is overtaking your file cabinet, give this a try: Take all of your dinosaur materials out of your file cabinet and put them in a box labeled "Dinosaur Unit." In addition to your files, place all of your dinosaur books, plastic dinosaur figures, and everything else you use to teach about dinosaurs in the box. Store the box in a classroom cupboard or closet. When you're ready to teach your dinosaur unit all of your resources are in one place. The boxes that reams of photocopy paper come in are perfect "unit" boxes.

4 Do a major file cabinet tune-up every few years. Set a goal to go through five files every day before or after school. A strip of bright construction paper placed behind the last file you went through marks where to begin the next time. Ask yourself the questions listed on page 10 as you go through each file.

5 You need a file cabinet that is clutter-free and user-friendly. Get there by discarding unused items! Don't feel guilty about getting rid of things you don't use. Put your discards in the staff room in a box marked "Free." Your discards will become someone else's treasures. Your goal is to have a file cabinet that's filled with ideas that you can access easily and that you'll really use!

MANAGE YOUR MATERIALS

Don't waste another minute looking for something you need! Get rid of the stuff you've been hanging on to for years and still haven't used. Organize everything else so you can actually find and use things when you need them.

Teacher's Manuals, Plan Book, and Grade Book

Stackable plastic vegetable bins are wonderful organizers for your teacher's manuals, plan book, and grade book. Label the bins by subject, and store your manuals and other materials in them. Make sure to label a bin for your plan book and grade book. Once you're in the habit of using the bins, you won't waste time looking for your manuals again. (They also work well for storing different kinds of paper. Organize graph paper, writing paper, scrap paper, and colored construction paper into the different bins.)

Teacher Magazines

Put your magazines in chronological order, number them, and photocopy the table of contents from each issue. Number the photocopied table of contents so it corresponds with the number you wrote on the front of the magazine. As you receive new magazines, number and photocopy the table of contents. Highlight the ideas you can't wait to try. Sort your photocopied pages into three piles—fall, winter, and spring. Staple all the fall photocopies into a folder labeled fall magazines. When you plan, use the indexes you created. Scan the photocopied tables of contents, and then easily access the magazines you need.

Games, Puzzles, and Math Manipulatives

Keep your eyes open for products that come in sturdy containers that you can use to store small objects in your classroom once they are empty. Ask parents to save containers for you. Some grated cheeses come in clear reusable containers perfect for math manipulatives.

Supplies

Look in an office supply store for plastic caddies with handles and compartments. They are usually sold next to the cleaning supplies. Fill the caddie with your stapler, extra staples, scissors, tape, pens, and pushpins. It's so handy to grab the caddie when you need to bring supplies to a meeting in another teacher's room, or to the office.

Poster and Chart Storage

The next time you visit a teacher supply store, ask whether they have any of the empty boxes in which charts are shipped. Cut off the top of the box to expose a few inches of your posters and charts. Tab each poster and chart with a sticky note for a label. Thumb through the tabs to quickly find the poster or chart you want.

Or, roll your charts and posters and clip them at the top with clothespins. Write the title of each chart or poster on the clothespin, using a marker. Store the rolled charts and posters in an empty trash can or large plastic pail.

Art Supplies

A hanging shoe bag is an excellent organizer for your art supplies. Look for a shoe bag with clear pockets. Hang the bag on a wall in your classroom. Sort through all of your art items, and pop them into the pockets. The shoe bag organizer is perfect for paintbrushes, pipe cleaners, glue sticks, colored pencils, markers, glue gun and extra glue cartridges (for teacher use only), cotton balls, craft sticks, brads, and so on. At a glance you can see through the pockets to find the items you need. It's easy to tell when supplies are getting low and need to be restocked.

Is your yarn collection a tangled mess? Collect large plastic soda bottles. Rinse them out and cut off the bottoms of the bottles. Slide a skein of yarn inside each bottle and feed the end of the yarn through the neck. Slip the cut-off end of the bottle into a plastic bag. Secure the plastic bag to the bottle with masking tape or a rubber band, then stack the bottles inside a cupboard or box.

Making the Most of the Reproducibles

Photocopy extra sets of these reproducible pages so you have brand-new ones ready to go.

Instant Jot-a-Notes
Sign your name on the "From" line on all four notes before photocopying. Copy, cut out, and store in envelopes or in your Notes to Write folder. Your presigned notes are ready to use!

page 17

Who Borrowed What?
Missing items are oh-so-easy to track down now! All it takes is a quick glance at this handy list. Staple a copy inside your Pending folder.

page 18

To-Do Lists
Lists help you instantly organize and focus! Keep these lists in a special spot on or near your desk. Stash extra lists in your Do Today and Take to Meetings folders.

page 19

Essential Phone Numbers
Create instant access to phone numbers with this handy list. Keep the completed list inside a Phone Calls to Make folder.

page 20

Communication Log
When it's time to document contacts with parents, you'll have all the information you need! Place extra copies of the log in a Phone Calls to Make or Notes to Write folder.

page 21

pages 22 & 23

Year-at-a-Glance Planner Plan your whole year! Tape together copies of these forms and jot ideas for units, long-term projects, themes, activities, holidays, and field trips on this instant overview.

Our Classroom Wish List
Instant notes come in handy when you want children to bring materials from home.

page 24

Information for Substitute Teachers
Attach lesson plans to this organizational form.

page 25

Field Trip Organizer
Field trips just got easier—you're ready for anything and everything!

page 26

❀ Thank You! ❀

_____
_____
_____
_____
_____
_____

From _____
                    Teacher

❀ A Note For ...

From _____
Date _____

_____
_____
_____
_____

Important Note

From _____
Date _____

_____
_____
_____
_____
_____

✏ A Reminder

For _____
From _____
Date _____

_____
_____
_____
_____

Who Borrowed What?

Who?	What?	When?	✓ Check when returned

Must-Do List

for _____
      (day)

☐ 1 _____
   _____

☐ 2 _____
   _____

☐ 3 _____
   _____

☐ 4 _____
   _____

☐ 5 _____
   _____

☐ 6 _____
   _____

☐ 7 _____
   _____

☐ 8 _____
   _____

☐ 9 _____
   _____

☐ 10 _____
   _____

To-Do List

(day) _____

TOP PRIORITY

1 _____
   _____

2 _____
   _____

3 _____
   _____

IMPORTANT

1 _____
   _____

2 _____
   _____

3 _____
   _____

DO IF TIME PERMITS

1 _____
   _____

2 _____
   _____

3 _____
   _____

Essential Phone Numbers

This list belongs to _____

Name	Number

Doctor _____

Pharmacy _____

Dentist _____

Car Repair _____

School Phone & Fax _____

Communication Log

Type of Communication (Note/E-mail/Phone)	Date	Who	About

Year-at-a-Glance Planner	September	October	November	December
Language Arts				
Math				
Social Studies				
Science				
Themes				
Field Trips				

January	February	March	April	May	June

Our Classroom Wish List

Teacher _____ Room _____

Please help make our wishes come true by donating any of these items to our class:

_____   _____

_____   _____

_____   _____

_____   _____

_____   _____

Thank you!

Teacher _____ Room _____

Please send these items to school if you can. We need them for upcoming classroom activities.

Thank you!

_____

_____

_____

_____

_____

Information for Substitute Teachers

Welcome to _____ Grade, Room _____

Locations

Lesson Plans/Schedule: _____ Grade Book: _____

Seating Chart: _____ Class List: _____

Emergency Information for Students: _____

School Emergency Procedures: _____

Helpers

Responsible Students: _____ and _____

Colleague: _____ is in room _____

Special Duties This Week

Monday _____

Tuesday _____

Wednesday _____

Thursday _____

Friday _____

Classroom Procedures

Taking Attendance: _____

Lunch Count: _____

Collecting Work: _____

Restrooms: _____

Recess/Lunch/End-of-Day Dismissal: _____

_____

Other: _____

Nonroutine Appointments for Students

Monday _____ Tuesday _____

Wednesday _____ Thursday _____

Friday _____

Extra Information _____

_____

Have a great day!

Thank you,

_____ , Teacher

Field Trip Organizer

Place: _____ Address: _____

Contact person (name, phone number, e-mail): _____

_____

Depart school: _____ Arrive: _____ Leave: _____

Transportation: _____

Adult supervision: _____

_____

_____

Students need: _____

_____

Costs

Transportation: _____

Admission: _____

Other: _____

Notes

Take along:

_____

_____

_____

_____

_____

The Number System

It's amazing how this system saves time and helps you and your students be more organized than ever before. Use a class list and number the names on the list from 1 to 25 or more. Here are a few ways to use the Number System—you'll find even more!

- Stick a small piece of masking tape on the upper right corner of each student's desktop. Use a felt pen to write each student's number on the tape. Have each student write his or her number on the upper right corner of all papers including homework, tests, and worksheets. This enables you to arrange the papers in numerical order to make sure they've all been handed in. You can record grades quickly in your grade book, because the numbers follow the sequence of your class list.

- Give each student two clothespins with his or her number written on each. Students can use them when they have to stop working in the midst of a project. They can clip everything together and place the pieces on a countertop. Now all the projects are numbered so you know to whom they belong.

- Use the numbers to pair up students with partners or to form small groups. Just list the numbers on the chalkboard.

- Have students number their folders and place them in a storage box in numerical order. Now children can quickly find their folders without having to look through the whole box.

- Number mailboxes in which students place things they need to take home. To sort folders or papers into the mailboxes, arrange them in numerical order and pop them in the mailboxes.

10 Time-Wise Tips

1 Focus on one spot at a time. Pick one conspicuously cluttered table, countertop, or desk to clean up, and get busy!

2 Sort your things and papers into three piles: put away, give away, throw away.

3 Set a timer for 15 minutes of "Organizing Time." Select your target and get going! You'll be amazed at how much you can accomplish in a short time!

4 Don't overextend yourself! Offer to share extra duties or committee positions with another teacher.

5 Establish a specific place for everything—for example, a hook on your desk for keys. You've instantly eliminated frustrating searches for important items.

6 Streamline your at-school errands. For instance, combine dropping off library books with a trip to the office.

7 Create In and Out Zones. Pick a permanent spot in the classroom where you place items you need to take home. At home, designate a spot to place everything that goes to school. Now you can zoom out the door!

8 Make the most of every minute at school. Lighten the load of work you take home by spending one short period each day working in your classroom. Ten minutes a day equals 50 minutes a week. Hang a "Teacher at work—please do not disturb!" sign on your door and go for it!

9 Simplify everything you can. Step back, scrutinize, analyze, and simplify lessons and activities. Always be on the lookout for ways to cut your workload. It's amazing how many ways you can find to work smarter, not harder, without compromising how much children learn.

10 Share the workload—plan units with a teacher pal at your grade level. Plan and prepare materials for an upcoming unit for both classes, and have your teacher pal do the same for a different unit. Congratulations—you've cut your work by 50 percent!

10 Great Ways to Stay Organized

1 Create a Sort & Put Away box or basket. When you have books, magazines, and papers in hand, don't pile them on your desk. Pop everything in the box to sort and put away later.

2 Handle papers *one time* for maximum efficiency. Sort mail near the recycle bin. Toss unwanted mail in the bin, and place items you want to read in your Read Later folder.

3 Sort magazines into boxes according to seasons. For instance, fall magazines all go in the Fall Projects/Activities box. When you need ideas for back-to-school, go through the fall box of magazines for ideas. If you look through a magazine and do not see any ideas you want to use, bring it to the staff room for others to use.

4 Start an Up for Grabs box in the staff room. Put magazines and materials you no longer want in this swap box. You get rid of clutter, and others have access to "new" materials.

5 Keep an eye out for baskets, boxes, crates, and other containers to use for storage and as organizers. Use cardboard boxes until you find the perfect containers for all your materials.

6 Create a Busy Box to stash papers that need to be folded, cut, collated, or stapled. Write directions on sticky notes. When a helper has a few extra minutes, he or she can tackle a task from the Busy Box. When a teacher friend stops by to chat, grab the box and work on no-brainer busywork tasks as you visit.

7 Label the cabinets and drawers in your classroom with numbers. Make it easy to direct students, helpers, and substitutes to your materials. It's so quick to say that math manipulatives are in cabinet #6 and art paper is in drawer #4!

8 Look in "dollar stores" for colorful plastic clips for clipping batches of papers. They're usually magnetic, so you can use them to clip reminders to your file cabinet. You'll use these handy organizers daily.

9 Try to keep your desk organized at all times. Use tape to label spots where things go.

10 Create a Found It! box where students can place puzzle pieces or manipulatives they happen to find in the classroom. On classroom cleanup day, one of the jobs can be to place items back in the box they belong.

10 Ways to Kick Off the School Year Right

1 List everything you do to get your classroom ready for a new school year. Add to the list as you prepare for back-to-school. Save the list to use again and again! This ready-to-go list instantly focuses and organizes you for a new year.

2 Label file folders with students' names, and place them in the front of your desk drawer. Use these folders to keep important samples of children's work and copies of notes from parents. Photocopy any notes you send to parents. If you have a communication log (see page 21) for a specific student, place it in his or her folder.

3 Opt out of time-consuming interior decorating for your classroom. Think back to a teacher you remember fondly. Do you recall how the room was decorated?

4 Don't feel pressured to have every bulletin board picture-perfect. Mount background paper and borders and post a sign in the middle of the bulletin board that says "Under Construction" or "Watch This Space."

5 Keep last year's plan book at your fingertips—it's a handy reference. Reviewing last year's plans helps you allocate the right amount of time for lessons, activities, and units you plan to teach again. It's also a great source of ideas.

6 Carefully consider which committee or extra task you'll do each year. If it makes the workload lighter, vary your responsibilities from year to year.

7 Hang a clipboard and pen just inside the classroom door. When parents have an important message for you, they can jot it on the clipboard.

8 Make a School Library Books box to keep near the door and have students place books in it that need to be returned to the library.

9 Set a precedent! Keep interruptions to a minimum when you are working in your room before and after school and during breaks. Locate your desk where it can't be seen from the doorway. The more you get done at school, the less you have to take home!

10 Share responsibility for classroom organization with your students. Teach how to care for materials and put them away properly. Designate the last 10 minutes of the school day on Fridays as "Let's Get Organized" time. Get everyone involved so the room is all set for next week.

10 Terrific Tips for Back-to-School Night

1 Send home a reminder note with the day, date, and time of the meeting as well as your name, grade level, and room number. Let parents know if children may attend. Print your note on brightly colored paper!

2 Post welcome signs outside and inside the door, and include room number, grade level, and your name.

3 Have a sign-in sheet so you know who attended.

4 Have name tags for guests to fill out. Have adults write their names and students' names in parentheses on name badges—for example, Ms. Mary Lee (Tina Brown).

5 Reproduce your wish list (page 24) or jot it on the chalkboard.

6 Post jobs for parent volunteers on the chalkboard. Write a job description, including what the job is and how much time it takes. This is a perfect opportunity to recruit volunteers for at-home and at-school jobs!

7 Label important places in the classroom with colorful construction paper signs, such as "Our Library! Children may donate books to our library."

8 Display materials and textbooks. Make colorful signs to help parents understand classroom activities. "Math Books and Manipulative Materials: With these, your child does paper and pencil activities and uses concrete objects to understand number concepts."

9 Give visitors a copy of the school calendar to notify them of holidays, how to contact the school, and a list of items children should and should not bring to school. Share a general overview for the year.

10 Have a notepad and pencil handy to jot down important information that parents may mention. Write reminders about follow-up notes and phone calls you need to make.

10 Tips for Wrapping Up the Year Neatly

1 List everything you like to do to end the year. Save and reuse your list every year!

2 One month before the school year ends, label a file folder "Next Year." Whenever you get memos, calendars, or notices that pertain to next year, you have a place to stash them.

3 Do your students use folders to organize their work? Have them make sets of folders for next year's class.

4 Collect a sample of work from each child during the last week of school. Use these work samples for a back-to-school bulletin board to show your new students the kinds of work they'll be doing in your class. Put the bulletin board up during the last week of school.

5 Have groups of students go through the classroom library looking for books that need repair. Find a parent volunteer to take the books home over the summer and make the repairs.

6 Cover bulletin boards with background paper and add borders. Now you've jump-started all your bulletin boards for back-to-school!

7 Look back in your plan book at some of the activities you did during the first week of school. Start a folder labeled "First Week of School" and begin planning the first week.

8 Treat your students to a visit to the classrooms at the next grade level. If there are three different classrooms, visit a different one each day. Students love getting a peek into the grade-level classrooms they'll enter next year. What an easy, yet high-interest, field trip!

9 Have children each write a letter to an incoming student. Encourage them to offer all of the wisdom they have gained. The greeting might be "Dear _____-Grader." On the first day of school, pass them out to your new students. They love getting mail from the "big kids"!

10 Don't let yourself leave school until you've filed everything that you've thrown on top of your file cabinet. You're doing yourself a big favor by taking care of this at the end of the year. When you walk into your room at the end of the summer, your files are ready for you!